ISBN 978-1-334-42385-7
PIBN 10761396

Letters from A Self-Made Merchant To His Son

Being some of the letters written by John Graham, head of the House of Graham & Company, Pork Packers in Chicago, familiarly known on 'Change as "Old Gorgon Graham," to his son, Pierrepont, facetiously known to his intimates as "Piggy."

By

GEORGE HORACE LORIMER

Written in Gregg Shorthand

Revised Edition

Published by permission of
SMALL, MAYNARD & COMPANY, BOSTON

The Gregg Publishing Company

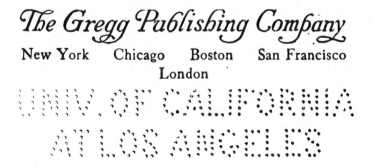

New York Chicago Boston San Francisco
London

Shorthand Plates Written by

Georgie Gregg

H-55-PP-5

Ch

PRIN[illegible]

ONE of the most interesting and helpful books published in recent years is "LETTERS from a SELF-MADE MERCHANT to his son," *by George Horace Lorimer.* We read these letters with much pleasure when they were appearing in serial form and made use of them—as did many other teachers—in giving advanced dictation to shorthand students. They were a welcome relief from the monotony of continuous dictation of business papers and correspondence, and at the same time they enforced many valuable lessons in such a way as to impress them vividly upon the minds of the students. The dictation of something in a lighter vein is desirable occasionally, and for this purpose there could be nothing more suitable than the letters contained in this book.

Recently William Marion Reedy, in an article about the *Saturday Evening Post,* which has been edited by Mr. Lorimer for many years said:

> George Horace Lorimer is the world's greatest editor. Lorimer's "Letters from a Self-made Merchant to his Son" is the best piece of pragmatic philosophy since Ben Franklin, who founded the *Saturday Evening Post.*

In issuing this selection of letters from the original book, we we desire to acknowledge our indebtedness to the publishers, Messrs. Small, Maynard and Company, for permission to use a certain number of these letters in this way, and also to the artists, B. Martin Justice and F. R. Gruger, for the use of some of the illustrations.

To those who enjoy reading these letters we heartily commend the complete work, which contains a number of others equally entertaining and helpful.

THE GREGG PUBLISHING COMPANY

CONTENTS

CONTENTS—*Continued*

No. 1

FROM John Graham, at the Union Stock Yards in Chicago, to his son, Pierrepont, at Harvard University, Cambridge, Mass. Mr. Pierrepont has just been settled by his mother as a member, in good and regular standing, of the Freshman class.

"Old Doc Hoover asked me right out in Sunday School if I didn't want to be saved."

I

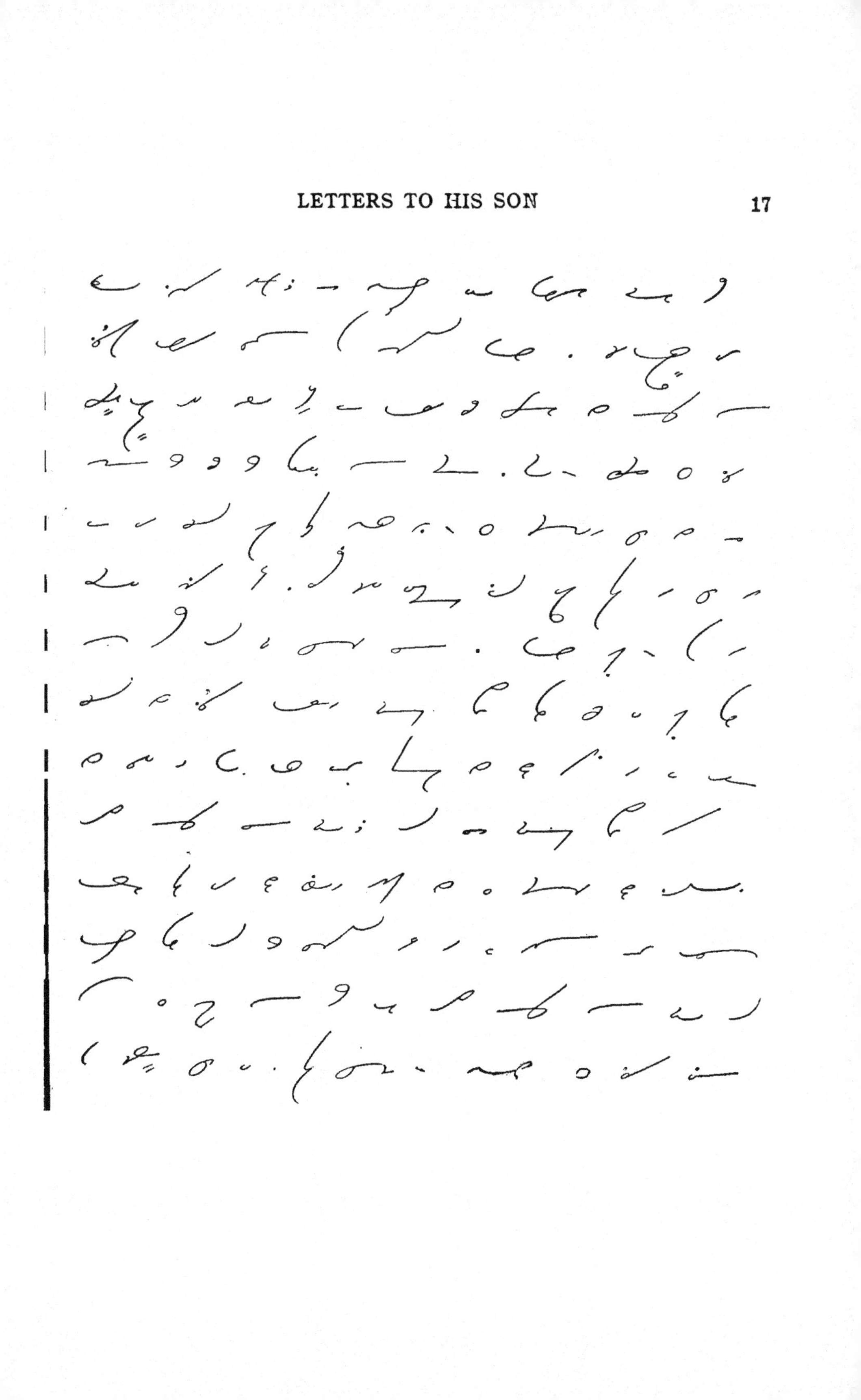

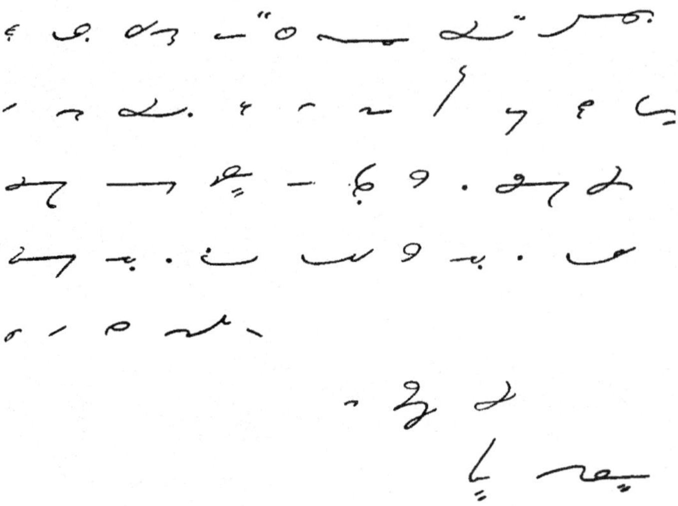

No. 2

FROM John Graham, at the Union Stock Yards in Chicago, to his son, Pierrepont, at Harvard University.

Mr. Pierrepont's expense account has just passed under his father's eye, and has furnished him with a text for some plain particularities.

"I have seen hundreds of boys go to Europe who didn't bring back a great deal except a few trunks of badly fitting clothes."

II

No. 3

FROM John Graham, at the Union Stock Yards in Chicago, to his son, Pierrepont, at Harvard University.

Mr. Pierrepont finds Cambridge to his liking, and has suggested that he take a post-graduate course to fill up some gaps which he has found in his education.

"I put Jim Durham out on the road to introduce a new product."

III

189—

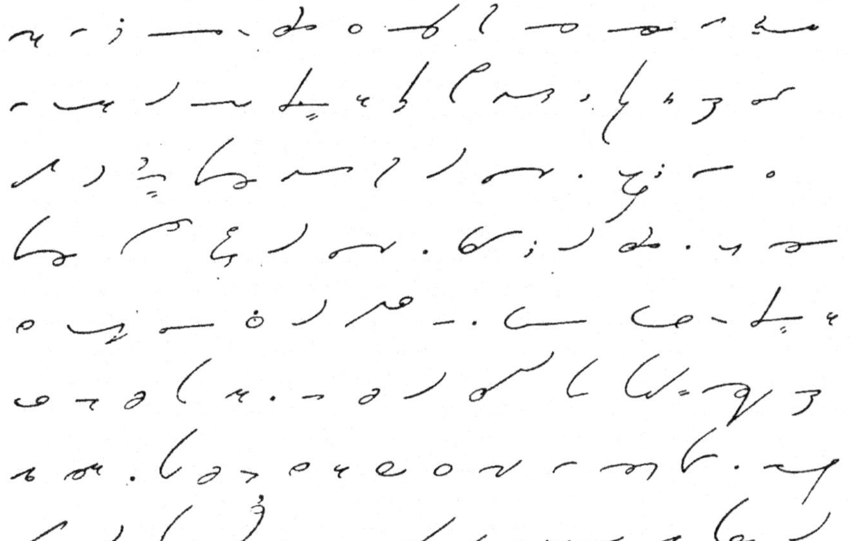

No. 4

FROM John Graham, head of the house of Graham & Co., at the Union Stock Yards in Chicago, to his son, Pierrepont Graham, at the Waldorf-Astoria, in New York. Mr. Pierrepont has suggested the grand tour as a proper finish to his education.

"Old Dick Stover was the worst hand at procrastinating that I ever saw."

IV

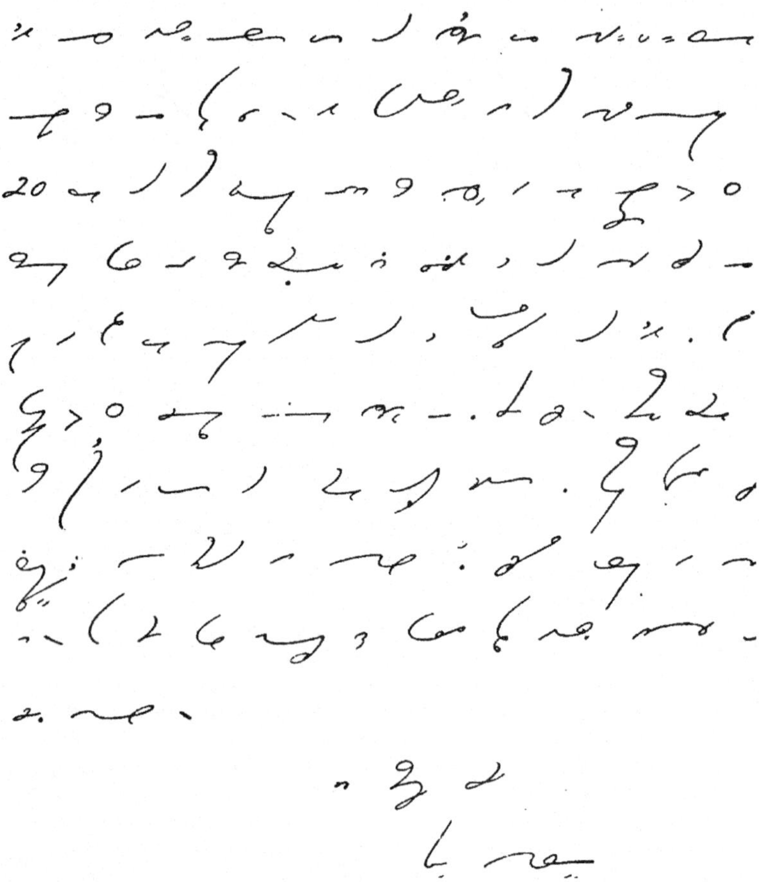

No. 5

FROM John Graham, head of the house of Graham & Co., at the Union Stock Yards in Chicago, to his son, Pierrepont Graham, at Lake Moosgatchemawamuc, in the Maine woods. Mr. Pierrepont has written to his father withdrawing his suggestion.

"Charlie Chase told me he was President of the Klondike Exploring, Gold Prospecting and Immigration Company."

V

No. 10

FROM John Graham, at the Union Stock Yards in Chicago, to his son, Pierrepont, at the Commercial House, Jeffersonville, Indiana. Mr. Pierrepont has been promoted to the position of traveling salesman for the house, and has started out on the road.

"You looked so blamed importe chesty when you started off."

X

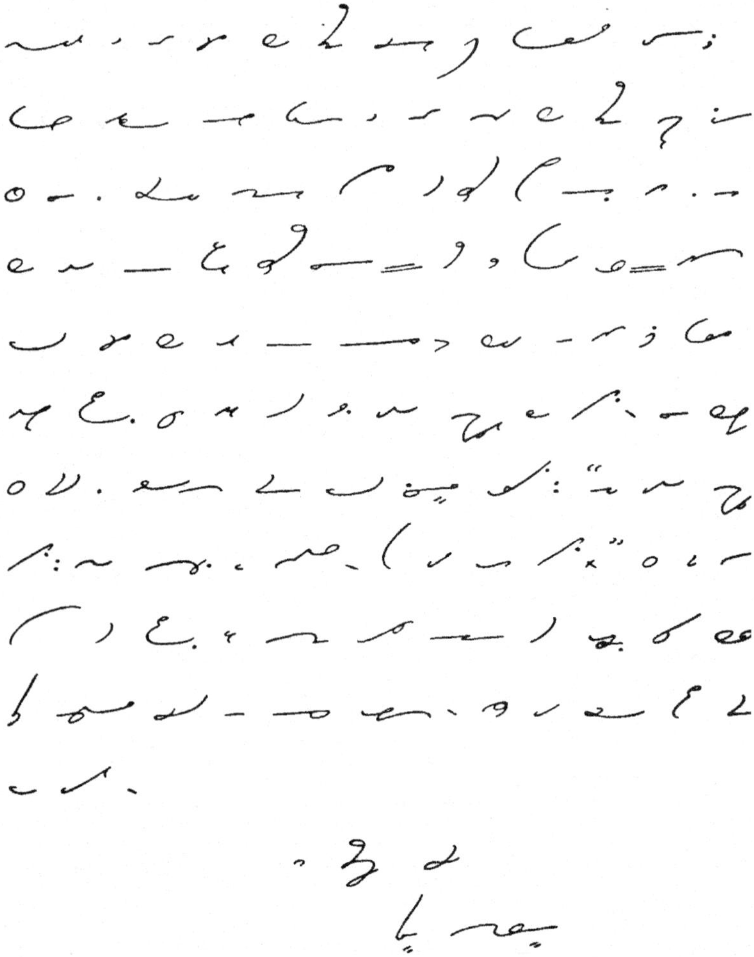

No. 11

FROM John Graham, at the Union Stock Yards in Chicago, to his son, Pierrepont, at The Planters' Palace Hotel, at Big Gap, Kentucky. Mr. Pierrepont's orders are small and his expenses are large, so his father *feels* pessimistic over his prospects.

"Josh Jenkinson would eat a little food now and then just to be sociable, but what he really lived on was tobacco."

XI

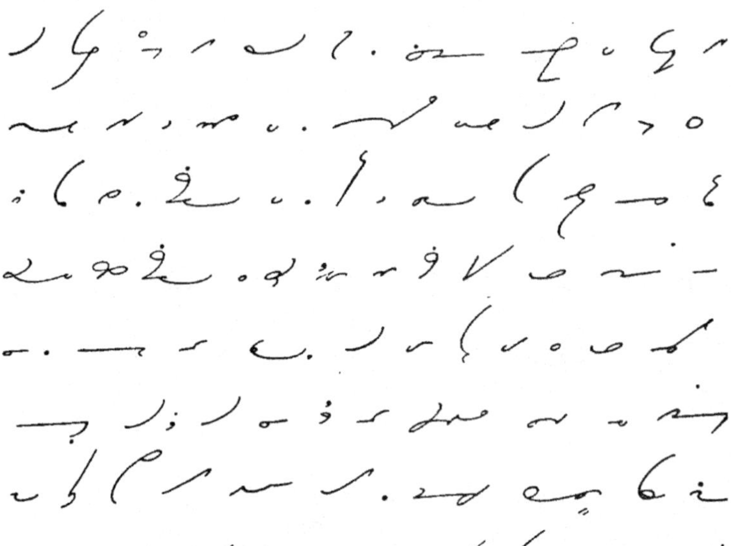

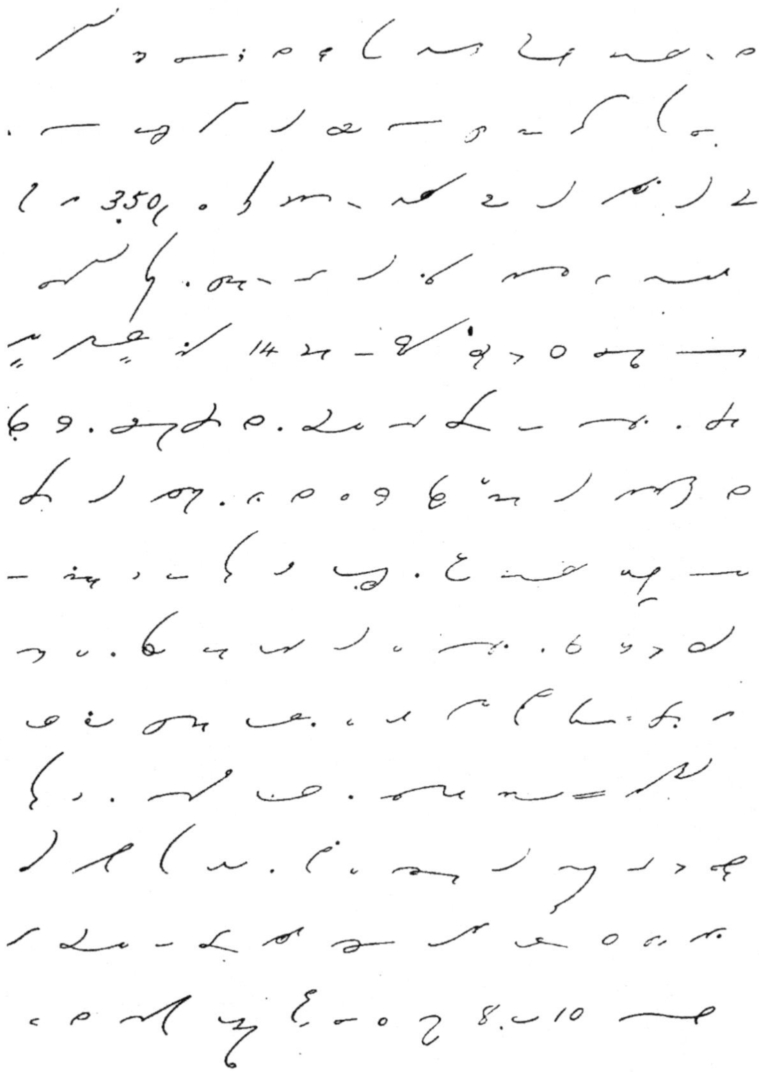

No. 13

FROM John Graham, at the Union Stock Yards in Chicago, to his son, Pierrepont, care of The Hoosier Grocery Co., Indianapo*l*is, Indiana. Mr. Pierrepont's orders have been looking up, so the old man gives him a pat on the back—but not too hard a one.

"When John L. Sullivan went through the stock yards, it just simply shut down the plant."

XIII

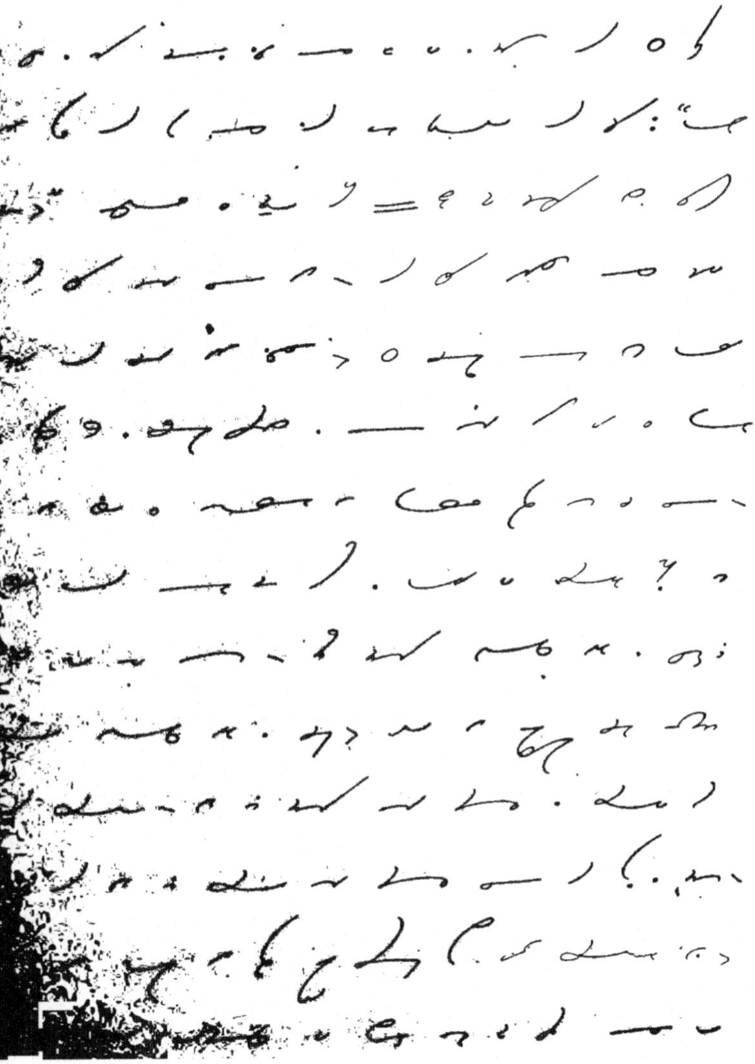

No. 15

FROM John Graham, at the Union Stock Yards in Chicago, to his son, Pierrepont, at The Scrub Oaks, Spring Lake, Michigan. Mr. Pierrepont has been promoted again, and the old man sends him a little advice with his appointment.

"A good many salesmen have an idea that buyers are only interested in funny stories."

XV

SOME GREGG PUBLICATIONS

(Prices subject to change without notice)

SHORTHAND INSTRUCTION BOOKS

Gregg Shorthand Manual. Revised edition. Bound in cloth... **$1.50**

Gregg Speed Studies. Combined supplementary textbook and dictation course, dealing with problems of speed and accuracy. All reading and writing material in shorthand, conforming to principles of the New Manual. 328 pages, cloth binding....... **1.20**

Supplementary Exercises in Gregg Shorthand. A collection of words, sentences, letters, tests and charts in shorthand and type, arranged in accordance with the division of material in the Revised Manual. 62 pages.............................. **.60**

Progressive Exercises in Gregg Shorthand. Revised for use with the New Manual. Tests students' knowledge of each lesson.. **.50**

Graded Readings in Gregg Shorthand. By Alice M. Hunter. A new reading book adapted to early dictation. 120 pages, cloth binding.. **.75**

Lessons in Shorthand Penmanship. By John Robert Gregg... **.12**

Gregg Speed Practice. Reading and writing exercises, combined with dictation practice. Illustrated with shorthand forms. 258 pages.. **1.20**

Gregg Shorthand Dictionary. New edition, containing the outlines of nearly 17,000 words. Flexible binding................. **1.50**

Gregg Shorthand Phrase Book. Contains about 2,400 useful phrases. A great aid in attaining speed. Vest-pocket size.. **.75**

Practical Drills in Shorthand Penmanship. By George S. McClure.. **.16**

Curso de Taquigrafia de Gregg. (An adaptation of Gregg Shorthand to Spanish.) Bound in cloth....................... **1.50**

Gregg Shorthand Adapted to Esperanto. By Ernest L. Jackson. Attractively bound.................................... **.40**

DICTATION

Expert Shorthand Speed Course. By Rupert P. SoRelle. Explains the methods and gives the practice matter used in training the successful contestants for the Miner Medal. 260 pages, bound in cloth.. **1.00**

Graded Dictation. By Walter Rasmussen. Carefully graded, with blanks for writing in the shorthand. 228 pages........... **1.00**

Shorthand Dictation Drills. Edited by John Robert Gregg. Carefully graded dictation material — business letters, literary and informative articles. Printed entirely in type. Bound in cloth. 212 pages.. **.80**

Constructive Dictation. By Edward Hall Gardner. Embodies a new idea of teaching practical business English along with dictation. Extensive vocabulary in shorthand. 376 pages. Cloth.... **1.20**

FOR THE REPORTER

The Gregg Reporter. By John Robert Gregg. A guide to court reporting, with list of reporting phrases and short cuts, plates of court testimony, etc. 111 pages, bound in cloth................ **$1.50**

Gregg Court Reporting Series. Practice matter on court testimony, jury charges, etc. **Gregg Notes Nos. 1 and 2** are the shorthand forms; **Gregg Dictation Nos. 1 and 2** are the transcripts. Each pamphlet.................................... **.24**

Gregg Reporting Shortcuts. By John Robert Gregg............ **2.25**

READING BOOKS IN GREGG SHORTHAND

Gregg Shorthand Reader. A collection of stories and articles.... **.28**

The Sign of the Four. By Sir A. Conan Doyle., 188 pages bound in cloth.. **.75**

Letters from a Self-Made Merchant to His Son. By George Horace Lorimer. Revised edition, 120 pages, bound in cloth..... **.75**

Creeds of Great Business Men. 38 pages.................... **.24**

A Christmas Carol. By Charles Dickens. 56 pages............ **.28**

The Great Stone Face. By Nathaniel Hawthorne.............. **.24**

The Legend of Sleepy Hollow. By Washington Irving.......... **.32**

Rip Van Winkle. By Washington Irving...................... **.28**

Hamlet. As told by Charles Lamb........................... **.20**

Alice in Wonderland. By Lewis Carroll. 154 pages............ **.75**

Advanced Practice in Gregg Shorthand. Three Parts. The shorthand version of the articles in "Expert Shorthand Speed Course." Each part.. **.50**

TYPEWRITING

Rational Typewriting. By Rupert P. SoRelle and Ida McLenan Cutler. Cloth bound, end opening.

Revised Edition. A comprehensive course for use in high schools and private business schools desiring an extended course........ **1.50**

Medal of Honor Edition. A short, intensive course for highly specialized business schools.................................. **1.08**

Methods of Teaching Typewriting. By Rupert P. SoRelle. Net **1.50**

Typewriting Speed Studies. By Adelaide B. Hakes.......... **.52**

ENGLISH, SPELLING

Applied Business English and Correspondence. By Hubert A. Hagar and Rupert P. SoRelle. Teacher's key furnished.

Commercial School Edition (exercises included). 344 pages... **1.40**

High School Edition (without exercises). 190 pages.......... **1.00**

Separate **Exercises** for use with High School Edition.......... **.40**

Applied Business Correspondence and Punctuation. 110 pages. **.75**

Separate **Exercises in Punctuation**........................ **.20**

Words: Their Spelling, Pronunciation, Definition and Application. A new idea in spelling texts. 162 pages, bound in cloth **.44**

OFFICE TRAINING

Office Training for Stenographers. By Rupert P. SoRelle. A complete and practical secretarial course for the advanced shorthand department, with separate Exercise Book. Text, **$1.25**; Exercises, 75c.. **2.00**

Inspiration and Help Twelve Times a Year

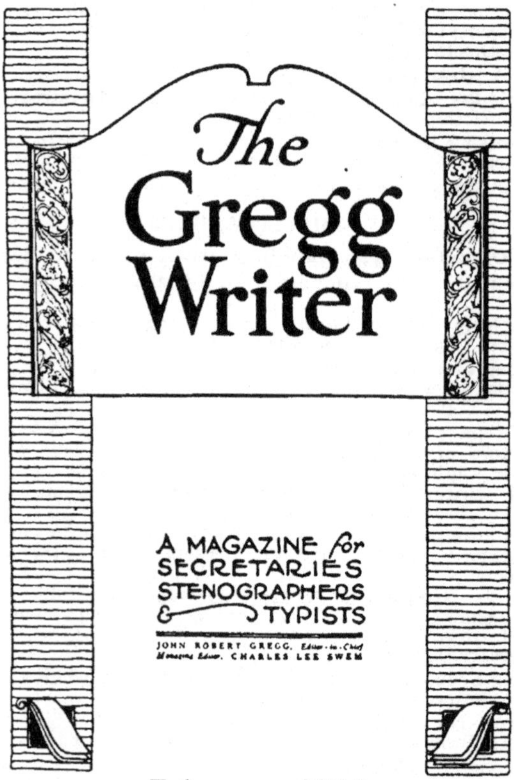

Price 15 cents **February, 1922** $1.50 a Year

Seventy-five thousand writers and teachers of shorthand study the Gregg Writer every month. "The Principles," the shorthand learner's department, the Art and Credentials Department, the Reporter's Department and the special articles and editorials are all packed full of information and inspiration for every stenographer, reporter, or teacher. The magazine contains from ten to fifteen pages of shorthand plates each month.

Subscriptions, $1.50 a Year in the United States; Canada and Mexico, $1.65; other countries, $1.75. Single copies, 15 cents.

Send all Subscriptions and Correspondence relating to the Magazine to

THE GREGG WRITER

631 South Wabash Ave. Chicago, Illinois

CPSIA information can be obtained
at www.ICGtesting.com
Printed in the USA
LVOW13s1659190617
538084LV00034B/622/P

9 781334 423857